THE HOTTEST SUMMER IN RECORDED HISTORY

THE HOTTEST SUMMER IN RECORDED HISTORY

ELIZABETH BACHINSKY

NIGHTWOOD EDITIONS

2013

Nightwood Editions
P.O. Box 1779
Gibsons, BC VON 1VO
Canada
www.nightwoodeditions.com

THE CANADA COUNCIL | LE CONSEIL DES ARTS
FOR THE ARTS | DU CANADA
SINCE 1957 | DEPUIS 1957

BRITISH
COLUMBIA
ARTS COUNCIL
Supported by the Province of British Columbia

Nightwood Editions acknowledges financial support from the Government of
Canada through the Canada Book Fund and the Canada Council for the Arts, and
from the Province of British Columbia through the British Columbia Arts Council
and the Book Publisher's Tax Credit.

This book has been produced on 100% post-consumer recycled, ancient-forest-free
paper, processed chlorine-free and printed with vegetable-based dyes.

TYPESETTING & COVER DESIGN: Carleton Wilson

Printed and bound in Canada.

LIBRARY AND ARCHIVES CANADA CATALOGUING IN PUBLICATION

Bachinsky, Elizabeth, 1976–
The hottest summer in recorded history / Elizabeth Bachinsky.

Poems.
ISBN 978-0-88971-276-8

I. Title.

PS8603.A33H67 2013   C811'.6   C2012-908224-4

To Friends

CONTENTS

It's why your silence is a kind of truth
Even when you speak to your best friend,
the one who'll never betray you,
you always leave out one thing;
a secret life is that important

—Stephen Dunn, "A Secret Life"

Now I am quietly waiting for
the catastrophe of my personality
to seem beautiful again,
and interesting, and modern.

—Frank O'Hara, "Mayakovsky"

YOU KNOW WHAT READERS LIKE
for Blake Smith

I can see now that I was once quite feral.
Getting older was my education in becoming civilized.

Also, being married to you. That was the decade
of cleaning our things in the nude so as not to ruin

our clothes with all the bleach. We couldn't replace
anything. When something broke, it was broken. We were

broke. I bought you a bullwhip and some hot sauce
and some tiny wooden armadillos and some tropical fish

magnets that wiggled when you opened and closed
the door to the fridge. You bought me a space heater.

Like Peter Q's Mrs. Bailey, I like to think "I had a strong
sense of what my position was and what was proper."

On two occasions, I shit myself: once when sick and
once when aroused. And here I'm thinking of Tess—

not the cat we sat, but the fictional girl
hanging from the fictional tree. I appreciated it

when you reminded me how easily I can become
bored. It's true. I do need a challenge.

A teenager is like a scarlet runner bean; it will wind
round whatever trellis you do, or don't, provide.

Sometimes it is satisfying to make a howling sound
that comes straight from the diaphragm. You know

what the diaphragm is? Ennui. The educated say
ennui. Your father is a machinist—I know what

he does, in theory—and you can build a train wreck,
though why anyone would want to build a train

wreck is unclear to most. I get it. Baby, we're
so private. And here I'm thinking of my grand-

mother in assisted living in Regina. Her TV
so quiet as to be imperceptible. The ghost

in her china. You are the first person I ever heard
say the word *hubris.* Your parents are social

democrats, your mother gave me Upton Sinclair's
The Jungle, and then I knew what Howlin'

Wolf meant by "The Killing Floor." You took me
for sushi. I bought a plastic harmonica

in the shape of an ear of corn. The first time
you licked my pussy, I was sure; the first time

you kissed my mouth, I wasn't. We did
everything backwards. You didn't seem to mind.

Often I would come home from my coffee
shop job and just sob. After so much violence,

it has become radical to be a soft critic, to write
poems about horses. I bought some glow-in-the-dark

zombie finger puppets and a plastic paparazzi playset
and an antique marionette in the shape of an ostrich

called My Favourite Pet. I hoped not to suffer from
what, in certain circles, is referred to as a "wet brain."

HORSE

for Michael Turner

For you, I'll recall
walking to the barn to ride my horse Biscuit.
1991. I wore a white blouse
that tied at the throat
and mom's brown leather coat
with tangles of suede
dangling from the sleeves.
I was thirteen.
See the camel-coloured
jodhpurs, the tall black riding boots,
my brown hair tied up in a pony-
tail, and me taking big steps
through the suburb?

It didn't take long to cut
out to the fields where
mom boarded the thoroughbred.
I went there after school,
but sometimes I'd arrive and
realize what I'd forgot,
so I'd tack him up and ride him back
through the subdivision
where horses couldn't go—careful
not to leave a hoofprint
on the neighbours' lawn.

I'd tie him to a streetlight
and go inside.

For you, I'd like to take
a picture of that. The empty
subdivision at 3:15 in the afternoon
on a Wednesday; those rows
of identical homes, brand new
as they all were then;
those pastel colours (you know
the kind) and the beige
vinyl siding and the brand new green
lawns like postage stamps
licked and stuck to the earth out front.
No trees, just a razed cow field
where developers built and
we moved in.

This picture is huge.
Pull back.
See my bay tied by the reins to the street lamp?

From here, he is small, impatient,
wanting to snip at the grass
with his enormous flat white teeth—
but he can't, he's caught up.
He lifts one wide front hoof and
brings it down on the asphalt,
a clop like two heavy blocks
coming together in an auditorium,
then stamps that hoof again—
my big dark horse, waiting
for me to come on back
outside.

WHO LOVES YA, BABY?

Eliot was right, it's useless to describe a feeling.
Much better to describe Silvermere Lake—
that shallow manmade lake at the mouth
of the Fraser Valley where I'm from.
Sometime, I'll drive you by it, the lake
with the island Telly Savalas owned then lost
in the '80s. I don't often think of Kojak,
but when I do I see Savalas standing
in a smoking jacket at the window of his island
home that overlooks Mount Baker and Iron Mountain
and the cool flat designer surface of Silvermere,
a lake three-feet deep at its deepest, ringed
with lilies, choked with ragweed, but real pretty
so long as you're not swimming in it or trying
to stand in the water. Here, your legs sink through
endless trucked-in silt fine as dust, slick with goose
shit. The smooth mud sucks at your feet till they pop
from the muck like corks at the shore. No Ithaca,
sir. No Catalina. But the kind of muck-hole
into which you could sink and be preserved
for eternity. Up the highway is where
the government dug for bodies in the runoff.
From here, you can chuck a rock at Blaine.
Go ahead and grow weed. The cops can't keep up.
But Internal Revenue will surely find you.

SOMETHING'S GOTTA GIVE

for Amber Dawn

Googling blondes is a pastime in which I partake
on especially lonely evenings. Their drug overdoses

interest me most, the blondes who've gone in similar ways,
sometimes mysteriously (the coroner can't find the pills, the booze,

whatever). Of course, some are still living, but there's a fragility
about these that reminds me of looking at a candle

through an egg, especially with their mouths full of expletives.
I prefer the divas. The ones with so much money

it's pickled their souls. What do they look like in the flesh,
I wonder? They are so beautiful and committed

to what they do—and, here, I'm thinking of Marilyn's
twenty-seven takes with a cocker spaniel, which required

patience and good humour. Such strange pale hair. I've
never seen it up close. What does it feel like? Clever girls.

DEBAUCHER'S TRIVIA AS VILLANELLE

What does it matter what you say about people?
What's the last word in A Touch of Evil?
—Jason Camlot, *The Debaucher*

What does it matter what you say about people?
If I'm up after hours, which bars should I know?
What's the last word in *A Touch of Evil?*

The biggest church? The tallest steeple?
When's the last time Kilimanjaro saw snow?
What does it matter what you say about people?

What tool do you use to jimmy a keyhole —
And once we're inside, where does Ann keep her blow?
What's the last word in *A Touch of Evil?*

What is a handshake a Mason might teach you?
Where is Dirty Dick's? What is Sloppy Joe's?
What does it matter what you say about people?

What to do with your hands when you peer through a peephole?
How much should I charge when Lou asks for a show?
What's the last word in *A Touch of Evil?*

In case of emergency, where can I reach you?
Tear off or unbutton? How slow should I go?
What does it matter what you say about people?
What's the last word in *A Touch of Evil?*

DREAMS
for Donato Mancini

It's another morning. Isn't that a good thing?
I do what I do every morning, I get up
from a dream. This morning it was a dream
in which I arrived at a dinner table filled
with poets I didn't know but who all knew me.
What a terrible feeling to be known by poets.
George Bowering says there are few things so boring
as other people's dreams. Still, we spend
a full third of our lives sleeping and some
of that, quite a lot, is spent dreaming.
Anaïs Nin says dreams are necessary to life,
but she is a different kind of writer. The kind
who writes *A Spy in the House of Love.* I
once dreamt I was making love to a man
who wasn't my husband after reading *A Spy
in the House of Love.* That was a lovely dream.
I would like to have it again. But what if
when Nin said dreams are necessary
to life, she meant that other kind of dream?
The kind that's like the sentiment you feel
when you look at the sunset over English Bay
on a clear June evening and you say, Oh,
that's just *poetry.* You don't mean words
on a page. You just need a word to describe
that thing that's going on out on the water.

I.M. 1

4:06pm: Elizabeth—*meep.*

4:48pm: Elizabeth—*any davey?*

4:49pm: Elizabeth—*calling davey...*

OTHER POETS' HOUSES

Living in houses lets me know
what it is like to live
in houses. The very best houses
(yours) have art on the walls
that I can look at and know
what it is like to look at real
art. Something real made
by someone real, framed
in a frame and hung on a wall.

When you invite me
for supper, I am busy talking
and can only glance at
what's on your walls. I don't
really see them—especially if
it's a poem in the frame—but
when I am alone in your house,
I can read what's framed aloud
and walk about and take

the dictionaries from the shelves
and drink the coffee from the freezer
and borrow a pair of slippers.
Slippers, coffee, dictionaries, houses
can hold a lot of books,
which is one good thing about
houses. And here's another thing.
One would think we'd be more different.
We think we are all different

and special but in fact we have
the same books and the same
coffee grinders and also the same
pots and pans. We are all reading
and then making decisions
about what we've read.
Are we wishing we were more
different? We like to put pictures
in frames and consider them.

We enjoy pictures—especially pictures
of our mothers and lovers. We have
computers and telephones and we keep lists.
We would like to live a very long
time please though sometimes
we don't live long at all.
The luckiest have the best views,
they look at an ocean or a pleasant
street or an intersected city: lights

on a harbour, the moonlight slicing
in through a dark window all lit up
and wow. I never know where the
light switches are. Thank you for
labelling them and also the water taps
Hot and *Cold* when they are backwards.
And your journals. They are all lined up
in a case with their wire spiral
bindings sticking out like spines: twenty

of them, fifty of them, a hundred of them,
a thousand. So many I couldn't bear
to open even one to snoop.
I don't need to. You write books.
If you have a garden, I'll look after it
for you while you are in Boston.
I am wearing a found bracelet. Don't worry,
I didn't find it in your house. And then
there are the things I can't discover.

Sometimes I want to look up. Understand
this living we're up to.

DEBAUCHER'S VILLANELLE FOR MUSES

for Peter Dubé

> *Missed the dead things at the museum.*
> *Had to go see about a carpe diem.*
> —Jason Camlot, *The Debaucher*

Missed the dead things at the museum,
The skin of a lion, the bones of an auk.
Had to go see about a *carpe diem.*

I went to take pictures, but just couldn't see them.
Couldn't focus my lens, hear the curator talk.
Missed the dead things at the museum,

Some convincing display, Clovis man and his woman
Crouched nude with their weapons in a distant epoch.
Had to go see about a *carpe diem*—

That feeling which blooms in the perineum,
That Neverland place at the base of one's luck.
Missed the dead things at the museum.

The stuffed and the painted and fixed, had to flee them.
My lover and I got the bathroom to lock—
Had to go see about a *carpe diem.*

Below, the dust stirred in that mausoleum;
While upstairs young William offered his cock.
Missed the dead things at the museum.
Had to go see about a *carpe diem.*

AT MOISHE'S, SAINT-LAURENT, MONTREAL

for David McGimpsey

What do I love to say? I love to say
We always do this. We always walk through
Mile End on a weeknight before supper and then you
and I go for steaks on Saint-Laurent and they
leave butter on ice and loaves of dark rye bread
and a dish of cold kosher pickles on a table
covered with white linen. I visit when I am able.
I say whatever comes into my head.
I say *I love this place.* Love the families
who come in wearing fancy suits and dresses.
There's a gold one. *A gold dress.* His
suit is good, I think. I can't tell if he's
rich. But tonight you've got money and so do I.
We always drink the wine and eat the rye.

SHARPENED PENCILS

for Zengetsu Myokyo

I have bought a box of sharpened
pencils, $2.29. What an evening
in Montreal! All by myself at Les Bobards,
having bought this lying box of pencils.
They are not sharpened! All twelve
of them—six blue and six red—all of them
dull and useless as screwdrivers.
I have had to beg a stub from the bar girl
who is French and does not know
the English word for *sharpener.* This
borrowed pencil, I hope, will make it
to the end of this poem. I should just go
for a walk up the mountain. I am an idiot!

My notebook boasts * 100 SHEETS * RULED
INSIDE COVER FOR USE AS A WRITING
GUIDE * FULL MONEY BACK GUARANTEE...
And I have just written on the ruled sheet.
Now I'll never keep my lines straight. This
stub, too, is starting to wear down; soon
I'll have no stub at all. What will Miss Barkeep
think now I've worn her pencil to nothing?
But, look! At last she has come with a sharpener!

NAILS
for Danielle Devereaux

I'm looking for a place that's just called NAILS.
There's always some place that's just called NAILS.
In every city and suburb, they'll do your NAILS.
They don't do waxing. All they do is NAILS.
Doesn't look fancy. Smells like NAILS.
Not a spa. No massage. Just your NAILS.
A gal talks smack while she files your NAILS
as the rain comes down outside like NAILS
on the roof of this place that's just called NAILS.
(You're in good hands. Just look at her NAILS!)
Where the working girls go to get their NAILS.
Where the travellers go to get their NAILS.
Have you seen this place? It's just called NAILS.
There's a neon light outside. Says NAILS.

I DROP YOUR NAMES

for Gillian Jerome & Jenn Farrell

When I read your poems
and see my name there
on the third line, balancing
like a teacup on the lip
of a ledge, and there is Gillian
on the fifth and Jennifer
on the sixth, I am moved
to tell you, please stop
putting our names in poems.
What do you think it will be like
reading this, or those, years from now
when you and I are gone,
or all but gone? It's been ten weeks
since we last met. Already
your faces are fading
from my memory like the periodic
table of elements or the
lyrics to some song I learned
while driving the Island Highway
one month I can't remember—
which is to say I can recall
those things well enough
to feel their absence and know
what's already gone.

LIONS GATE BRIDGE

for George McWhirter

You can see her from the sea. You can see cars
inch north and south under the gift of lights
a beer man gave to Vancouver's sky at night.
Strung tighter than a junkie at either shore,
she's nightmarish. The *idea* you can't get across;
slight; anachronistic; from a distance,
thin as a hair crawling with pestilent traffic.
But in the evening, cool air curls in through the narrows
and the traffic calms,
and lovers sit in one another's arms
at Prospect Point and behold her. How we love
to look at what we keep and what we have.
When she comes down at last, the future comes.
With it, other lovers. Other charms.

4:50pm: David—*Davey in the hizzy. How you, darlin?*

4:51pm: Elizabeth—*GREAT. I'm sitting by the ocean!*

4:52pm: David—*I'm sitting by a cable television. OK, you win. How's the book coming?*

4:53pm: Elizabeth—*I finished it yesterday. Now I am drinking wine.*

CHARGER

for Rick Tucker

What kind of car was that? The kind you used to drive
when we were kids and dated for a while?
You called it a muscle car. I never drove it.
It was standard and I couldn't drive standard yet.
Plus, you were six-foot-two. I couldn't reach
the pedals even when you'd ram the driver's seat
as close to the steering wheel as it could go.
You never drove it fast. You drove it slow,
but the engine grabbed whatever juice you gave
and gobbled it. You tapped your foot; it hopped.
For the next few years, my boyfriends hated you.
I'd remember. Tell them how we used to
love. Oh, wow. You broke my heart, remember?
The leather interior. The black dash. Was it a Charger?

JONNY,
for Jon Paul Fiorentino

We were travelling together,
so there were suitcases and a pair

of handcuffs. We were at some
school in a big city with _____.

I got some snail mail from _____
that I decided to give to you.

I got fired from _____
and the next time we hung out at

your apartment you gave me cocaine.
We made out in a park, then again

at a hotel where I hadn't been
staying. We snuck into the pool any-

way and dove off the diving board a few times before
we got kicked out for being "too queer."

I have the best dreams when
you are in them.

But then we also played Nicky Nicky Nine
Doors on Death (he was on floor 9).

We knocked
and knocked

then ran to the elevator and hit floor 2.
I sure do miss you.

PRAIRIE GIRLS

Talk sweet, but I know better—
They never share the rules by which they live.
The family's pure as sugar in the batter
And you can't taste, and they can't let you in.
Their men are making money in the fields:
Uranium and oil and diamond mines,
And money falls like rain upon their kids
And money fills their cups and kills the time.
And money comes to some and not to others,
And money buys them homes and things to eat.
And money makes Elizabeth a mother,
And money makes a favourite of Pete.
And money makes Elizabeth a mother,
And money makes a favorite of Pete.

PEREGIAN BEACH MALL PARKING LOT, PEREGIAN BEACH OZ

for Paul Magee

Paul, I admit
it was a mistake
to take your son
to pet the nice pit bull.
Especially since the child
had short sharp sticks
in either hand.

I was far from home.
Neither the child
nor the dog
belonged to me.

The dog was the colour
of a brindle cow
or an ocelot—an
animal that hopped
with pleasure

when I pet it. I deserved
the talking-to. It was
a good way for the boy
to get bit.

SALLY PERKINS

Always looking for something from everyone,
The man behind the counter at her café,
The man who drove the bus, the man, a man.
What she wanted she wanted from a man.
Her father. Wanted something from her dad.
Her teachers. Wanted something more from them.

Was she creepy? She was creepy. Poor them.
It seemed she wanted far too much. Everyone
agreed. Who was this creep? Who was her dad?
You could find her sitting quiet in her café
wiping her nose on a napkin, waiting for a man.
You could tell the little creep just wanted a man

from the way she wouldn't look around. No man
could get the girl to smile or look at him.
Hello, he'd say. But she knew it was a man
who called and so she wouldn't look, everyone
a threat. Still, she enjoyed her studies, her café.
Sometimes she sat and thought about her dad.

Who was he? Where'd he go? Who had her dad?
Who had his lap (her lap)? He was a man,
that was all. He could be anyone. Her café
simply crawled with him. She looked at them
sideways so that they wouldn't see, but a man
always knows when you are looking. *Everyone*

knows that, she said real quiet. *Everyone*
knows that's true. I'm so creepy. Dad?
Sometimes she sat and thought about some man
she didn't know, but wanted. Some kindly man
who'd take her in his lap, who'd quiet them—
all those bitches cruel in her café.

One day she cut her hair right off. Her café
burned. She got straight As. Everyone
saw her convene. It didn't mean much to them,
but she looked out and thought she saw her dad.
Her gown was long and black. She kneeled. A man
touched a baton to her forehead. Another man

held out her degree. *Talk to them, Dad,* she said.
Are you the man I saw at the café?
Be a man. Stand up. I want everyone to see.

DREAM OF AMERICA

In which I dream of bikini academia,
my flat-ironed hair smooth and soft as sun-

tan lotion slicked on my taut, perfect abs
which I flex on Venice Beach, one

perfect flex after another perfect flex
as I crack the perfect American book of poems.

I am brilliant as a collegiate smile. The weed, the sex,
central to my thesis. The palms

give me shade, cool my fierce beauty
which is angular and angry and knows just what it is worth.

And who is on that muscle beach with me
but stranger after stranger, each tall and tooth-

some? I bite. My lines American lines
because they sink right in. I can fly anywhere,

but it's you who fly to me, parched for limes
steeped in vodka, the breeze off the Pacific, my black hair.

7:37pm: Elizabeth—*OK. You should really be here.*
We could write sonnets by the sea. There are little seal heads
bobbing out there on the water. Right. Now.

7:37pm: David—*By now the seals have slinked*
away to be someone else's flipper pie. I would love to
sonnet by the ocean.

7:38pm: Elizabeth—*Hee. Now I'm stoned.*
Hee. Totally stoned.

7:39pm: David—*Rhyme "flipper pie" with "high." Totes!*

SOMEWHERE THERE IS SOMEONE WAITING

for Sheryda Warrener

To dislike this poem, to dislike me.
There are so many reasons to dislike me
and this poem. It really is astonishing,
how many. One thing, we do not rhyme.
Another thing, "I" am present.
I would like this poem to be a present.
I would also like this poem to rhyme.
There are many things to hope for in this world.
Somewhere, someone would like to tell me
"Repetition is not rhyme, Missy."
Astonishing. Poets like this word.
I like this word. I'll use it again: Astonishing!
How could you not like me? Not like this thing?

SLEEPING WITH JANE

for Thomas Ziorjen

Florence couldn't remember much because she had Alzheimer's
disease, so she moved into her daughter Jane's house—the house
her daughter shared with the son-in-law Florence had traditionally
disliked a great deal. Now she didn't know him and that felt better.
She didn't know the children, either. She thought the family bunny,
Spot, was a cat. Florence said, "What are you going to call that cat?"
"It's a bunny," her grandson said. "Bunny, That's a good name,"
Florence said. "It looks just *like* a bunny." The son-in-law, a stay-
at-home dad, looked after Florence during the day. "Who is that
man?" she asked her daughter one night. "I don't know him,
but he makes me a lovely breakfast and I think he's sleeping with Jane."

HOBBLED

for Donna Kane

A horse in hobbles *hops*. 1500 pounds of horseflesh,
hopping. It's unexpected! Surprisingly graceful,
too, they way they get over and around the deadfall
with this simple length of twisted rope fixed
in a mud-caked figure eight below the fetlock.
Without the hobbles, these horses will get far
from the place where we can find them easily
in a day; even hobbled, it takes us hours
to track them through this burnt forest of alders
where green shoots and wildflowers bloom
from the charred ground already green. We track
where their hooves have turned the earth,
where their droppings sit lightly on the ground.
We lose them, then pick them up again, this time
on the far side of fast-moving water we must cross
one at a time on a fallen log fifteen feet above
the water. This is the place we must consider
carefully, legs and arms can come apart, heads
can be bashed out on the rocks. How did horses pass
this place? This river, wild enough to pull us under,
is clean. But how clean is clean when it's moving
below you? Grazers, by nature, adaptive, adapted,
the horses have learned to eat willow, like deer.
We can see where they've stripped the leaves

from the branches with their delicate mouths,
where they've slumped into a soft bed of needles
to rest. Without the hobbles, they will return
in a perfect line all the way to the Chilcotin, back
they way they came, back all 900 miles nose-to-tail,
sipping willow along the way. We have lost them.
We have lost them again. They don't want to be found.

XMAS GIFT

This is the sonnet I wrote for you in Spain.
This is the sonnet I wrote in fifteen minutes.
No. Kidding! You get what you get when you
get it. *Get it? Do you get it? Do you get it?*
Do you get it? Do you get it? I probably know
more about this business than I should—
and that's why you should hire me. Think
of all the good I'd do around here, cleaning up
the iambs and putting away the gerunds
where they belong. I could also do laundry.
I'd know which gift I'd pick! This is the sonnet
I wrote for you in Vancouver. It is what
I could afford at the time, understand?
When are you coming over, anyway? Babe?

ARS ORATORIA
for Rodney DeCroo

NAMES

We are always getting names wrong, but that is because we meet so many people and are expected to remember their names. If we weren't expected to remember names, we would remember them. We've tried mnemonics and also face-to-name games, but we still can't remember a lot of them. Some names, we can remember. But mostly we can't. Especially the names of babies. Some of those names aren't even names. At least not names we've ever heard of. The names we are most likely to remember are the ones shared with our friends and family. It is nothing personal if we forget your name. We forget everybody's names but we are still quite generous in conversation. We know your face; that much is certain. And possibly also your occupation or any project on which you've worked. We remember your work, even if only vaguely, and even then we can't quite remember what it is called. Not exactly. Near. We can get near to the name of the thing you do. That isn't enough, but it is something. You can always tell if we can't remember your name, because we won't call on you. In conversation, we'll say, "Yes, you," or "This gentleman here," or "Hello, yes," and "What do *you* think?" It is all very vague. It gives the impression we don't care to know one's name, but that isn't it. We care. It is just we can't remember. It panics us to run into a person whose name has left our mind as swiftly as we've been told it. Important names; names of people who've given us money; people who've gone out of their way with kindness of some sort. The names of husbands and wives. We can never remember those. What are we doing that we can't remember any names, or that we don't have to? What kind of world is this? We aren't rich or beautiful. We are the kind of people toward whom some are inexplicably drawn. We give speeches.

is that when we are giving one, there are many more people watching us than we are watching. We make an effort not to watch them. We speak to the space just an inch above their heads. It looks as if we are looking at them, but we aren't. We are looking just past them. It is for their comfort. Especially those close to the podium, for whom the fear of being looked in the eye is especially great.

to help us remember people's names, but we can't remember their names.

UP IN THE 747

for Christine Bachinsky

When, for no reason, my sister leaned over and bit me, hard,
on the outside of my upper arm above my elbow. Hard
enough to leave a crescent-shaped mark identical to
the curvature of her rather large, white, perfectly shaped
adult teeth. "Fuck," I said. "That hurt." I stowed my magazine.
"I'm so sorry," she said. "I don't know why I just did that."
Below us, the well-combed provinces, buried under ice.

8:53pm: Elizabeth—*xo*

8:54pm: Elizabeth—*It's boring by the sea. There's nothing to do.*

8:54pm: David—*No TV?*

8:55pm: Elizabeth—*Nope. Just podcasts and a wicked internet connection. And a lot of books.*

8:57pm: David—*That's okay then. The howling of the wilderness can only be stalled with inexpensive access to pornography.*

8:57pm: Elizabeth—*It's either that or Alice Munro.*

8:59pm: David—*Or some strange combo born out of Canada.*

WHEN I HAVE THE BODY OF A MAN

When I have the body of a man, I have the head of a bull.

When I have the head of a bull, Athena springs from my forehead.

When Athena springs from my forehead, I tell Athena, *Cut it out!*

When I tell Athena, *Cut it out!* she makes a string of paper dolls from
    my money.

When she makes a string of paper dolls from my money, I say *Thank
    you,* fold them up, and put them in a drawer.

When I say *Thank you,* fold them up, and put them in a drawer, the
    dolls figure out a way to get out and use eBay when I'm not home.

When the dolls figure out a way to get out and use eBay when I'm
    not home, I know I've not had enough to drink.

When I know I've not had enough to drink, I admire my fortitude.

When I admire my fortitude, Athena says, cut it out!

When Athena says, *Cut it out!* one should always listen.

When one should always listen, I think, *Don't tell me what to do with
    my time!*

When I think *Don't tell me what to do with my time!* I have the body
    of a man.

ON AEAEA

after Jeramy Dodds

She turned that man to a sailor called
by Circe: all swine and snuffle on some
godforsaken rock he couldn't swim from
since he didn't know his talents; stuffed

his face in her skirts till all he could see
was his snout doing the gods' own noble work—
holy *moly*, he tore it up.
It couldn't last. When that boy turned,

he turned, shall we say, from slack
to full. The costume dropped and beneath
rose a man to take her down. *Okay*, she
said. *Okay, boss. Take it back.* He took it back.

THE HOTTEST SUMMER IN RECORDED HISTORY
(A FICTION)
after Charlotte Bronte's Villette

Lisa Snowe was staying in her dear friend Jonny's rented apartment
in Montreal, an apartment belonging to Leonard Cohen. This was after
Cohen lived in California and became a Buddhist and carried on
with that young model (I forget her name) and after he'd lost
millions to a corrupt manager and now, supposedly, owned
only shitty, yet charming, flats in the Plateau just off Saint Denis.
Miss Snowe was reading Jonathan Ames and eating alone
in the evenings since her husband was committed to working
summers and could not join her in what was supposed to be Canada's
most romantic city, or at least Canada's most licentious city,
and everywhere it seemed there were beautiful young women walking
with their men and it occurred to Miss Snowe that she, being plain,
was not one of them.

Jonny was off in Russia and had recently written to complain
that his girlfriend, a young law student, was visiting her mother in
Albania and that Russian women were impeccably dressed, forlorn,
and terribly attractive. What was he to do but return to his bug-
infested hotel room for an equally forlorn "tug" as he was
so fond of naming the act of self abuse. So Snowe was feeling
feverish and thinking about the handsome lesbian couple
with whom she had spent the previous evening in conversation
about poetry. The taller girl, like a gentleman with sleek dark eyes,
walked Snowe home. They walked slow or, rather, she walked
slow as they walked slow and spoke of adultery; had Miss Snowe
committed it, would she commit it, and Snowe had to say no.
No, she had not and would not,

not in nine years of cohabitation though, on occasion, she had
been tempted. There was the tall red-headed girl at Yaddo
with whom she'd shared a moment in a rock garden and also
the tow-headed boy with whom she had admired the tea roses;
both of them met on a trip supposed to allow her the luxury
of sitting and thinking and writing, but most certainly not
fucking, and she thought how sad! How completely sad.
Jonathan Ames, you dig so deep. Only days before, she'd given
a performance at an outdoor festival in Toronto. That night, it had rained
but, by the time Miss Snowe stepped onstage, the stars had come
out and so had the fireflies. She heard her first cicadas
sizzling like a power station.

In Toronto, Miss Snowe stayed at a B&B on St. Peter's Street
not far from the University. The poet R_____ was there and also
a well-known book filmmaker from New York. R_____ let Snowe
join him for breakfast on the *balcon.* A thunderstorm flashed around them
and he spoke of the holocaust museum in Berlin. He made gestural
movements over his croissant and she felt she must truly go
to Berlin. The filmmaker was not as she expected. Only a few years
older than she, he did his best to align their life experience, though
Miss Snowe still envied his Harvard education, his exotic
childhood in Tennessee, his doctor father, and his mother
who only ever needed a high school education. He had the kind
of body that looked as though he spent many hours at a gym
in Brooklyn. She did not

find the filmmaker handsome, but she did find him delightful,
especially when, once late at night, drunk, he called her Ma'am.
"Yes, Ma'am," he said. That night, they shared a cab and made
their way back to the B&B. It was very late and Miss Snowe wanted
to sleep. But, when she went to her room, the power went out.
She sat in the dark. It was humid. She was alone. Why did she knock
on the filmmaker's door? Surely he would not answer, but he did.
And when he did he was nude to the waist, and so neatly made.
She thought she would like to kiss him. But, of course, she couldn't.
What must he think of me? she thought. *This awkward woman
waking him to tell him the power has gone.* So she slunk away
to find a breaker and, as she passed him, said "What does it matter?
All I need to see is the back of my eyelids."

Earlier that summer, she'd fallen for a novelist from Detroit
whose wife was three months pregnant and ran a sausage shop
in Boston. He was an ugly man, but Snowe had a love of ugly men.
All the ephemeral friends had left the party and they were alone.
He'd been a soldier in Iraq and now he was writing about the war.
Snowe ordered him to lace her boots, which he did, and he stayed,
and she wished him luck with his baby. "Yes," he said, and held
his hands about a football's length apart. "They're about this big," he said,
and then he left and she thought: *Ridiculous. What is this? Life is pitiful,
yet somehow still worthwhile.* Miss Snowe wanted to thank him,
to thank *him*. But for what? She could think anything. And now, here
she was in Montreal, away from home and before her stood little
Sophie, nineteen. Little Sophie

with her long legs and her longer brown hair and her amputee boyfriend
who'd lost all the fingers on his right hand though,
fortunately, not the thumb. What a sight to see, him rolling
cigarettes out front of the Copacabana with his stump and his thumb
and Miss Snowe standing there, married. Married like her dear
Jonny had been married. Jonny who couldn't live with his wife
because he couldn't stop fucking other people. "I was married
nine and a half years," he wrote from Russia. "But I fucked this person
and then I fucked this other person just after my daughter was born.
It's pretty common..." and Snowe knew it to be true. She had no daughter.
At home, in Vancouver, it was thirty-nine degrees. The hottest summer
in recorded history.

THE MOUNTAIN

after A.M. Klein

Who knows it only by its ragged edge which cuts
into the daylight hours its milkwhite teeth
knows its shadow;
and who from a passing train knows its peaks—
which rise vertiginous from the frozen land,—
holds in her mind a mountain.

In layers of mountains the history of people,
and in this ridge,
which daily from a commuter's train I find
from a distance, my youth—
the green taste of ferns, taste of cedar,
grey hard field of stones beneath the skin of water—
O all the blue-white evenings
are still to be found.

There is a campground, near the waterfall,
where bottlecaps like those I flipped with wicked thumbs
upon my mind still flash their rounds of silver.
And the falls, like a monument adorned with nude bathers,
still run where playing lovers
Jonny and I tested caresses there
(with occupation flinging away our guilt)
against its flat grey smoothed-out precipice.

And all my Augusts there are black and neon-green
like the bodies of garter snakes undulating slim in shadow
beneath the weightless colour of living leaves, dark green, green,
    and yellow
rooted in earth, and threaded
throughout the fir trees above the turbulent water—
cover and canopy of youth,
a teacher's presents.

And blackberry summer cloying purple on my tongue!

The burnt car lit by the silver Zippo still
rests in the leaves by the trailhead lot where I
one evening in September watched boys
grow dark, the wood quiet, then suddenly spill
from canisters their kerosene, then their spark, then the light—
terror and holiday!

One of these days I will go up to the second falls
to see if it is still there—
that cool electric stone
where,—as we listened to the river's rush
made bright and to our mood by the moon and its proximity—
the boy I loved
loved me.

8:59pm: Elizabeth — *Alice Munro porn. Hot. How would it go? Starts out on a remote Ontario Island-on-a-Lake…*

9:00pm: David—*Hateship, Friendship, the Pizza Guy and a Boat.*

9:00pm: Elizabeth—*Heh. Yeah. Like that.*

9:03pm: David—*The Lives of Girls and Women and More Girls—Really Hot Girls.*

9:03pm: Elizabeth—*Who Do You Think You Are (Up My Skirt).*

9:04pm: David—*Ha!*

9:05pm: Elizabeth—*God, I'm BORED!*

WHEN YOU FIRST MEET A DOMESTICATED DOG

He is a frightening prospect, indeed.
There's the slavering mouth full of teeth,

and the hair that stands up like bristle.
It noses your crotch and takes a good snuffle

and—what's this?—it wants a little pet?
Everyone seems okay with that,

standing around eating chicken off the BBQ
like there isn't an animal among you.

OCCASIONAL POEM FOR BILL BISSETT, AUGUST 21, 2011

> happeeness is sew tempting yu
> dont want 2 fall apart if yu don't
> get it.
> —bill bissett, "Pavlov's Dog I"

The first poetry books I ever read were bill bissett's
at the Maple Ridge location of the Fraser Valley
Regional Library in BC and I thought it was THE GREATEST
POETRY because I loved how the words were all over
the place and spelled wrong and the pages seemed
so mysterious to me. I didn't know much
about Canadian Poetry. I was fourteen and I couldn't
spell terrifically well, I don't think. Then I saw bill
read at the Sunshine Coast Writers Festival
when I was sixteen and it was THE BEST READING EVER
because for the first time I knew that poetry could be
something really TRANSCENDENT and EXCITING
and I knew there were poets out there being poets
for real and living and reading what they wrote
to lots of people in big venues like the Rockwood Centre.
For a long time I wrote like bill in my diaries especially
when I was eighteen and nineteen and living in my car
and travelling all around America that way. Later,
when I had become a "real poet" and was so depressed
and living in New Westminster in 2002, Billeh said
*I know what will cheer you up: you should meet bill
bissett.* I noticed bill called everyone miss or mister.
And some people were royalty. So me and Billeh
and bill all went to see a movie called *Spellbound*

—a documentary about children's championship
spelling bees—and bill spelled all the words in the dark
along with the kids. It was so great to hear him
spelling like that, although I think he found it stressful
watching those kids have to spell on command.
It really is a very stressful movie. That was almost ten
years ago. Sometime later, bill invited me to visit him
in the West End to look at his paintings. He had just
broken his arm and was making these very one-armed
paintings that looked a lot like letterforms and marks,
very simple, very painful. I stayed and cleaned up
his dishes a little because he really couldn't do much
except make those one-armed paintings. I remember
using the little yellow sponge and looking out
the small kitchen window, and thinking how could
he do his dishes with a broken arm and I was really
quite worried about him. When I invited him to read
at the Maple Ridge Arts Centre where I was artist
in residence years later he said YES! And all he asked for
was tiny mouthwashes and the Dutchess brought
his paintings out from Vancouver and we filled up
that black studio theatre with those paintings and
a lot of them were SO GREAT I wished I could buy
a big one but I couldn't. Most of the Maple Ridge
town councillors were there and also many elderly
ladies and about eighty other people and bill chanted
a lot over and over, *I don't want to suck Empire
I want to suck you…* Now Blake and I have two
of his paintings. One of two man-trees-with-cocks-
or-vaginas in the blue woods and another he painted
after that time he shattered his shoulder playing
hockey and the marks are red all over and it looks
like it really hurt to paint it. I think the marks look

like vaginas. So much of what bill writes about is sex.
I APPRECIATE THAT because I too like sex and writing
about it and bill also likes to write to and about
his friends which is also something I like to do
all the time. I do it a lot thanks to bill. Blake and I
have a lot of bill's books and publications *sailor;*
peter among th towring boxes; lost angel
mining company; seagull on yonge street; MEDICINE
my mouths on fire. Awake in th Red Desert is
A REALLY GREAT RECORDING, and a whole lot
more. We love them because there is a lot of history
in them: the history of Canadian places and people
and if you ever want to be reminded of how some
people would really rather poets got "real jobs"
instead of getting grants from the Canada Council
you can just think of bill. Did you know bill was
the Conservative Party's poster boy for eradicating porn-
ography from Canada Council-funded art in the '70s
and that was really hard for him and then later on
people like Molly Starlight got called out for much
the same thing with her chapbook *Where Did My Ass Go?*
That was not that long ago, maybe eleven or twelve
years now and we can expect that sort of thing again
soon, I think. I don't write so much like bill anymore.
I write like me. But I still always think about bill
and his EXCELLENT poems. Sheri-D Wilson has even called
him a Shaman and says once he visited her bird
when her bird was sick and after bill spent some time
with that bird, it got better pretty much right away
and stopped picking its feathers out with its beak.
It got better because bill is MAGICAL. I wonder how
bill gets away from the autocorrect on his word processor.
It must be so annoying for him to work on a PC or a Mac.

One more thing: I've been lucky to be able to read
with bill sometimes when I am travelling. I think
I've got to do that at least four or five times now
if you include today and last month at the Whitehorse
Poetry Festival where the Gold Rush Inn caught on
fire and had been BURNING FOR QUITE SOME TIME when
bill wandered down into the lobby like it was nothing
at 2am and it was still light out and he gave me a Halls
cough candy, which was great because fire is stressful
and Halls are so soothing. Later that week he even
called Blake on our wedding anniversary because my
phone wasn't working and I was so lonely and bill said
Blake… where are you? Happy anniversary! It's 11pm and it's bright as day…
which was such a relief because for a while when bill
wasn't so well he kept getting Blake's name mixed up
and he thought Blake's name was Drew, so sometimes
Blake still goes by Drew. We love bill so much.

ELEVEN THINGS TREENA COULD LIFT AFTER EMERGENCY SURGERY TO REMOVE A THIRTY-TWO-POUND FIBROID TUMOR

for Treena Chambers

Sixteen full-grown gerbils

Eight Mars bars

Sixteen baby chicks

Chihuahua puppy (three weeks old)

At least one hundred gerbera daisies (flower tops only)

One newborn polar bear cub

Half a September *Vogue*

Ninety quarters ($22.50)

One cup of tea

$450 dollar bills (any denomination)

THIS IS HOW
for Billeh Nickerson

This is how to tell about the end of your life but not the poem.

This is how to pass your days away.

This is how to enjoy your office.

This is how to walk across the street.

This is how to be specific.

This is how to make a movie.

This is how to make your mother say *balls.*

This is how to make a giant mess.

This is how to solve all the problems of all the world.

This is how to arrange an arranged marriage.

This is how to attend a Weight Watchers meeting.

This is how to call your friend whose left eye has filled with blood.

This is how to text your friend in Montreal.

This is how to keep your clothes on.

This is how to recall her curly orange hair.

This is how to work a room.

This is how to board a plane.

This is how to wonder where the money always goes and it goes on booze.

This is how to cultivate friendships with underdogs.

This is how to befriend only the paranoid.

This is how to lose your own damn mind.

This is how to keep every moment.

This is how to make your sister a gift for Christmas.

This is how to explode your journal.

This is how to wield a sword. A real sword, fool.

9:05pm: David—*What kind of liquor did you bring?*

9:07pm: Elizabeth—*Bottle of wine tonight. I ought to go get a bottle of scotch. I should have brought a good bottle of scotch… grrr. And all the board games in the cabin are for two people.*

I could sit here and pretend I'm two people…

9:09pm: Elizabeth—*… or I could hassle you all freaking night.*

COLD CALL

My phone rang and reminded me, *Have a baby.*
Who knew there was a setting for that?
There was a tomato in my pocket.
I was walking to Sheryda's house on West 13th.
We say house when what we mean is apartment.
Sheryda is pregnant.
We ate waffles from *Patisserie Lebeau*
with Greek yogurt and seasonal berries.
This, we ate in her sunny kitchen.
This was the end of summer in Vancouver.
(We say summer when what we mean is less rain.)
I went to the shoe store to exchange my new boots
for the same boots in a larger size.
They didn't have my size.
I returned the boots.
In the fall is when our mothers bought us
the one pair of shoes that would last us all winter.
New shoes mark the beginning of the school year.
Remember jelly shoes? They cut into your feet all summer.
I called my husband and said, "I returned those boots."
"It's going to be okay," he said. I wasn't.
Sheryda wants to know about cool.
What's cool? The inference being
it ain't us. You can get an organic hot dog sans
nitrates on Granville Street near The Bay.
Neither Sheryda nor I really understand America.
Nine months earlier my phone must have whispered,
Get pregnant. Where was I walking then?

I WANT TO HAVE A CHUCK AND DI PARTY LIKE MY
PARENTS DID IN THE '80S

for Jamella Hagen

But where will I get the helicopter?
And who will make my dress
out of garbage bags for me? And where
will I find the two-by-four and a good-sized
rock for our game of rockball?
And how will we climb the ridge
to the glacier? And who will dig
the trench to the fuel pump? And where
will we get the klieg lights? And who
will decorate the army cots
with fluorescent tape? And which forest
might accommodate us? And who's got
a big enough van? And who'll bring
the eucalyptus? And which river will
be cold enough? And where will we get
the lumber? And who knows how to build
a sauna? And how long will it take to grow
our beards? And who's got a canoe?
And who can lift it into the helicopter? And
how will it fit? And who can fly the helicopter?
And then what will we do with it?
What about the caribou and the siksiks?
We'll need a rifle just in case. Last year there
was a grizzly bear. Last year there
was no night. Last year we got in trouble.
Last year we wore hula skirts. Last year
we lost Arden, then found her. Last
year we looked through binoculars. Last

year the kids played in the iron tailings.
Last year Frankie blew up the pumphouse.
Let's not do that again! Let us not eat
Wonder Bread, let's eat bannock.
Let's eat ham with scalloped potatoes
and also some of that saskatoon berry jam.
Let's cook with mom in the trailer
let's swing from the beams in the bunkhouse.
Let's hold the fossils the geologists found.
Let's hold the geologists. O, white night
of northern remembering, let your still light fall
on the faces of your partiers. The elders say
the sun is not coming up where it should.
What does this mean for meteorologists?
What does this mean for us?

THE SPIDERS' ALPHABET

for Jan & Crispin Elsted, Barbarian Press

Once in rural Japan my good friend Allan joined a fascinated throng
    in watching a white spider meander across a market square,

a white spider whose body was fat as a man's hand and whose slender
    legs tested the earth as a woman's might test the surface of a lake

mid-May—then it moseyed. And when I first moved from the city
    to the woods outside Vancouver, I evicted two from my laundry

room, an old married couple, bodies each a good inch long, grey-brown.
    They were pissed. They lived without a web. They were hunters,

the whole length of their basement window replete with corpses:
    fat blackflies, millipedes. A real nice set-up. I screamed!

But all summer in the press room, I have watched a thin brown thing spin
    webs behind the type cases. And I have thought of E.B. White,

his Charlotte, and what I would do with my Charlotte after she,
    feeling safe, spun her pale yellow sac near the small window

that opens onto your derelict English garden. I watched the sac hatch
    and for weeks afterward I found spiderlings among the ligatures.

We worked together. Me, dissing type while the little ones wove
    through the alphabet. Now—the wolves who stalk through

my house at night?—they keep my tabby entertained.
    In the day, I leave my windows open, and my doors. Yet how

pest-free my house remains! Some nights I dream of eight eyes and wake
    to unexpected cash. Strange. This fall when I move back to

the city with its silverfish and exorbitant rent. I think I will summon
    spiders. It is best to live with them. To let them into the house.

BIRTHDAY POEM, 2012

The birches went a long way back.
You couldn't see past them.
They were planted in rows.
We'd better look out for that bull,
I thought. My sister agreed.

We could see it stamping one
cloven hoof way off in the distance.
Just a little brown bull, far off.

Then it came charging.

A bull is a terrible creature.
Its horns are terrible.
Its eyes are terrible.
Its solid flesh steams in winter air.

We'd better get behind this tree, I thought.
My sister agreed and the bull got bigger
as it came closer until it slammed into us, into our tree—then

that furious thing
backed up and started over again.

I'll admit I was frightened,
but my sister was laughing. The way you might in church
or a particularly earnest high school
presentation.

It's not her fault.
I am my sister, the forest, the tree.
I am the bull
and the still-frozen ground.

No sound.

Shoulders moving
up and down.

MERE ANARCHY, ST. JOHN'S NFLD.

for Stephen Ferrone

> *Turning and turning in the widening gyre*
> *The falcon cannot hear the falconer;*
> *Things fall apart; the centre cannot hold;*
> *Mere anarchy is loosed upon the world*
> —William Butler Yeats, "The Second Coming"

When my plane touched down, I was disoriented.
They buried Shirley's mother that day, but I hadn't met Shirley yet.

Across town, Lannie was eight months pregnant—
a boy's back against her spine, her stomach hard

as a tabletop, pupils so dilated you could fall into them
if you weren't careful—and Marie was raging like the North Atlantic

seething, surging, roiling water come up hard against what was
once Africa now fused to North America.

I was a tourist. No. I was a visitor and I was dreaming
the bad dreams of an addict who's just coming to.

Up ahead was the only traffic jam the rock would see for weeks
and I was behind it—one silver truck full of gear backing up

into the loading bay of the Mile One Centre, the real Mile One
way up on Signal Hill and out a little farther two French Islands

and a kind old sweet fella with dementia to whom I'd reintroduce
myself every twenty minutes. I didn't mind. I couldn't remember

who I was either. I forgot how to work. How to do my laundry.
How to eat. It was easy to forget and it kept getting easier.

I had several excellent ideas, none of which I wrote down
and a handful of desperate students marched up and down Bond Street

banging pots and pans in solidarity with other desperate students
in Montreal. All I wanted was to be beautiful and tidy. All I wanted

was all new friends and to supply such applicants with a New Friend
Questionnaire to make sure we shared the same sense of humour.

A Vietnamese philologist did my nails in a place called NAILS
and I knew I had come home and would continue to do so.

Downtown, roadies unloaded lights and the Blind Boys of Alabama
led each other in a line and got ready to sing "Way Down in the Hole."

I said, "I am particularly good at doing what I am told," but I was lying—
and the BBC told us Venus was in transit in front of the sun.

Next day was the Queen's Diamond Jubilee and a stadium rose
around me. Ten thousand voices. And I listened.

What didn't break? What did? Two mugs (cracked). A desk
chair (broken). Ring on the countertop (stained). Cutting board

(warped by water). Toilet (chain snapped) like I was too rough
for the place and things wouldn't stop breaking and I knew my thinking

was out of sorts when I thought of Yeats and his falcon and his falconer
and couldn't fathom the hand that held the bird. All I knew

was that some force was passing overhead and I was under it.
And there was Shirley, too, burying her mother and Lannie picking out

the right receiving blanket—the one with the monkeys because
it was classiest—and Marie, missing all her teeth, still raging, raging,

hanging on to a chair, her anger hot as a laser and looking for whom?
    For me?
Out-of-towner. From Vancouver. And, oh, god, life was strange

but I went out to meet it. I didn't know what I didn't know:
that we could look out for each other. But *look out* for each other!

Look out, b'y, the townies said. *Look out!*

ACKNOWLEDGMENTS

"Debaucher's Trivia as Villanelle," "The Hottest Summer in Recorded History," "Debaucher's Trivia for Muses" and "At Moishe's": *PRISM international*
"The Hottest Summer in Recorded History": *Forget*
"Other Poet's Houses" and "Horse": *CV2*
"Sleeping With Jane" and "Dream of America": *Eleven Eleven*
"Up in the 747": *Nthposition*
"The Alphabet and the Spider": *Matrix*
"Hanging Caps" and "Prairie Girls": *Riddle Fence*
"You Know What Readers Like," "Dreams," "When I Have the Body of a Man" and "Who Loves Ya, Baby?": *The Fiddlehead*
 "Sally Perkins": *West Wind Review*
"The Fire," "Cold Call," "Jonny," "I Drop Your Names," "Sharpened Pencils" and "Peregian Beach Mall Parking Lot ...": *death hums*
"This is How," "Cold Call" and "I Drop Your Names": *Arc*

"Lions Gate Bridge": *Verse Map of Vancouver* (Anvil Press)
"Occasional Poem for bill bissett" was written for *The Vancouver Queer Film Festival, 2011*
"I Want to Have a Chuck and Di Party Like My Parents Did in the '80s," appeared in *Arc* magazine and as a broadside (House Press, 2010)
"The Mountain," written in the style of A.M. Klein, appeared in the chapbook *The Mountain* (Synapse Press), which is a companion text to *Failure's Opposite: Listening to A.M. Klein* (McGill-Queens University Press, 2011).
A line from "Sharpened Pencils" appeared on a limited-edition pencil for Kalpna Patel's *Pencil Project,* Toronto

I am grateful for residencies at the University of the Fraser Valley, the Banff Centre for the Arts and the Muskwa Kechika Artist Camp, and an apprenticeship at Barbarian Press. I am also grateful to the Queensland Poetry Festival, which brought me to Brisbane in 2009, the Scream in High Park in Toronto, and to the Montreal Zen Centre. Many of the poems in this book were written in, or about, these places.

"Other Poet's Houses" is for Silas White & Amanda Amaral (Pender Harbour), Rob Hughes & Jenn Farrell (Mayne Island), Meredith & Peter Quartermain (East Van), Lee & Ed Gulyas (Bellingham, Washington), Darren Bifford & Iris Simixhiu (Montreal), Andreas Schroeder & Sharon Oddie Browne (Roberts Creek), Stan Dragland & Beth Follett (St. John's) and Zengetsu Myokyo (Montreal) — thank you for allowing me into your lives and homes. Darren Bifford, Jenn Farrell, Lee Gulyas, Gillian Jerome, Matt Rader, Nick Thran and Sheryda Warrener commented on early drafts of the manuscript. I am grateful for your advice. Love to Dave McGimpsey for letting me run our I.M. throughout the book and to Sachiko Murakami, Cathy Ahlers and Stephen Ferrone for being angels on this earth. Blake Smith found the book. Billeh Nickerson pulled it from the fire. Love. To the British Columbia Arts Council and the Canada Council for the Arts, thank you.

ABOUT THE AUTHOR

Elizabeth Bachinsky is the author of five collections of poetry: *Curio* (2005), *Home of Sudden Service* (2006), *God of Missed Connections* (2009), *I Don't Feel So Good* (2012) and *The Hottest Summer in Recorded History* (2013) Her work has been nominated for awards including the Pat Lowther Award and the Governor General's Award for Poetry. She was born in Regina, raised in Prince George and Maple Ridge, B.C., and now lives in Vancouver where she is an instructor of creative writing and the Editor of *Event Magazine*.